Let your imagination take flight when you come to RAMM.

RAMM's exhibits will spark conversations about the past.

At RAMM you can meet the real thing face to face.

Welcome to RAM

Museums are places where people c of objects. Visitors can learn a lot froi.. can stimulate our creativity and spark new ideas. At RAMM, people, objects and ideas come together to help us understand and acknowledge what happened in the past and contemplate the challenges of our future.

Every object entering the museum comes with its own tale to tell. And just like our stories, they include episodes that are inspiring and uplifting, as well as ones that are traumatic and difficult to talk about. Whatever their back-story, all of RAMM's objects are treated with care and respect.

Explaining where an object comes from, who collected it and why, can raise difficult questions. RAMM was created when Britain was a major colonial power controlling the lives of millions of people around the world. Some collectors abused their position and took without permission. Others treated the people and wildlife they encountered with respect.

While history is often presented as a single version of events, really the past is made up of many different stories. RAMM is constantly uncovering new ones that have been lost or hidden. They cannot all appear in the galleries, so they are used as the content for websites, social media posts, temporary exhibitions, talks and events.

RAMM is an Exeter City Council service, and entry to the museum is free. We appreciate your support and donations.

We hope you enjoy your visit.

ROYAL ⋅ ALBERT ⋅ MEMORIAL

Contents

History of RAMM

RAMM's distinctive façade – a mosaic of local stone – has been a much-loved Exeter landmark for over 150 years. Its architect, John Hayward, was inspired by medieval churches to include arches, columns, tracery and even a rose window. His design captured the Victorians' love of the Middle Ages in the style known as Gothic Revival.

The distinguished Victorian politician Sir Stafford Northcote was the driving force behind the foundation of RAMM.

The original design for the museum included an ornate central tower. This was never built due to its cost and the planning permission it required.

RAMM's distinctive façade has been part of the landscape of Queen Street in Exeter since 1868.

The 21st-century redevelopment created a new extension and garden entrance.

In 2018 RAMM marked the 150th anniversary of its public opening. It was celebrated by a Carnival of the Animals through the streets of Exeter.

There were calls for a museum in Exeter from the 1840s, but it was not until 1861 that the project gained momentum. In that year, Prince Albert's death led Devon MP Sir Stafford Northcote to launch an appeal for a local memorial. The result was a proposal for a building on Queen Street to house a museum, art gallery, library, art school and college, named the Devon and Exeter Albert Memorial Institution. The first phase was completed in 1868 when the public opening was celebrated by a 'Grand Bazaar and Fancy Fair', concerts and a banquet to help raise more funds.

The museum's storerooms were soon overwhelmed with collections, one of the most important arrived in 1868 from the Devon and Exeter Institution. The need for more space led to expansions through the 1880s and 1890s. After the 1899 extension was opened by the Duke and Duchess of York, the Albert Memorial was granted the right to add 'Royal' to its name. In the 20th century, some of the institution's functions – library, college and art school – moved out and the building became known as the Royal Albert Memorial Museum or RAMM.

From 2007 to 2011, RAMM underwent a major redevelopment, primarily funded by Exeter City Council and the National Lottery Heritage Fund. A new gallery, entrance and courtyard were designed by the architectural firm of Allies and Morrison. In 2012, RAMM won the Art Fund prize for Museum of the Year.

DID YOU KNOW?

RAMM is just one of many buildings and places named after Queen Victoria's beloved Consort. Others include the Royal Albert Hall, and Victoria and Albert Museum in London, Lake Albert in Uganda, and Mount Albert in New Zealand.

The Courtyard

With well over one million objects in RAMM's collection, the large display case in the Courtyard is equal to less than 0.01% of the total. This floor-to-ceiling display gives a glimpse of all of RAMM's collecting areas: Antiquities, Costume and Textiles, Fine and Decorative Art, Natural Sciences, Numismatics (coins and medals), Social History and World Cultures. The case is a giant cabinet of curiosities, like the displays that were created in the earliest types of museums.

Wooden, 17th-century, **pulpit panel** showing Abraham preparing to sacrifice Isaac. This panel was collected by Harry Hems who ran a successful architectural carving business in Exeter. The collection was displayed around his workshops to inspire the workers.

The **Dawlish Bronze Age hoard**. Gold bracelets, broken bronze weapons and fragments of bronze ingot were buried around 3,000 years ago in marshy ground. Who did this and why?

DID YOU KNOW?

Sedan chairs, like the one displayed here, were a popular method of transport in the 17th and 18th centuries. It enabled the wealthiest in society to reach their destination without getting their shoes and clothes ruined by the dirty streets.

This museum

Case Histories

Meet Gerald the giraffe. Come nose-to-trunk with an African elephant. Listen to someone playing the harpsichord. Imagine trying to carve two tiny figures on a grain of wheat!

Case Histories is a meeting place for objects and stories from across the world. How did they all end up in this museum? Some exhibits were given to RAMM by people who collected them while living and working abroad. Others were found in Devon and Exeter.

We recognise that collectors in the past often did things that a museum would not do today. For example, we certainly wouldn't accept an elephant

that someone had recently killed for sport. Yet, wherever they came from, all these objects were given to RAMM for the same reason – so that people could experience and study them at first hand.

Every object has its own story, opening a door to other times and different places – maybe close to home or in distant parts of the world. Gerald is still the only giraffe you're likely to meet in Exeter!

A tiny hand-carved **wheat grain** was made at the Japanese temple complex of Ise Jingū. The deities are representations of the Shinto gods Daikokuten, and Ebisu. They are often seen together as the deities of bountiful harvests.

This **meteorite** is around 4.5 billion years old – the oldest object in RAMM's collection.

Czigane the **Siberian sledge dog** accompanied Robert Falcon Scott on the 1910-13 British Antarctic Expedition to the South Pole. Scott mentions this dog several times in his notes. Despite falling very ill on 22 October 1911 Czigane made it back to the UK safely.

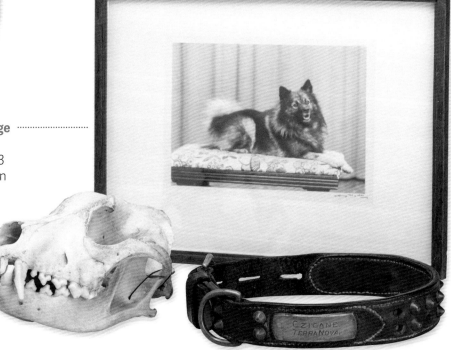

Curtius leaping into the Gulf is one of RAMM's largest paintings. In legend, a giant chasm once opened up in the centre of ancient Rome. Marcus Curtius persuaded the gods to close it again by jumping in and sacrificing himself.

Finders Keepers?

In this gallery you'll meet some of the men and women who gave their collections to RAMM. These gifts helped to establish the museum's world-class collections of objects, from prehistoric flint tools to rare shells and Devon lace.

The methods of many 19th-century collectors were very different from modern standards. Collectors were fired by curiosity and wanted their collections to look as impressive as possible. They sometimes killed birds and butterflies simply for their beautiful colours. They didn't always give much thought to conserving natural habitats or recording information about where and how objects were found.

Today we are more interested in how objects relate to the places they come from. We want to know what the objects in this museum can tell us about how environments and ways of life have changed around the world.

For example, RAMM's shell collection contains extinct species that can no longer be studied in the wild. These museum specimens provide important information about the effects of climate change on habitats and ecosystems. This is one of many ways in which history can shed light on our future.

In the late 18th century, the East India Company sought to exploit and export India's valuable natural resources. It employed Indian artists to make detailed drawings of plants and animals, which became fashionable for collectors. Renowned artist Bhawani Das, ভবানি দাস, created this **painting of sea holly** used to treat headaches.

This piece of **carved caribou antler** is a tactile map of the coast. Inuit hunters attached maps made of wood or bone to clothing, worn round their neck or held inside mittens. The shape of the carving represents landmarks and distances helping them navigate after dark.

Many of the **Hawaiian tree snails** in Juliana Linter's shell collection are now critically endangered or extinct. They are vulnerable to habitat loss and predators introduced to the islands by humans. Hawaiian tree snails do not lay eggs, instead they give birth to just a few live young each year.

Once there were between three and five billion **passenger pigeons**, making this one of the world's most abundant birds. Yet over a period of just 400 years they were hunted to extinction by humans.

Charlotte Treadwin's great skill as a **lace** maker earned her a Royal Warrant in 1848. Numerous royal commissions and **prize medals** followed. She exhibited at the Great Exhibition of 1851 and the International Exhibition of 1862. Charlotte ran her Exeter manufactory on very modern lines. She paid her workers a fair wage in cash, rather than in goods.

Not all of RAMM's stories are easy to listen to. **Charles Peel** spent his life travelling the world to hunt mammals. Some of this museum's favourite exhibits were presented by Peel.

This white **silk evening mantle** was made in Japan around 1905 for the western market. Its rounded neckline, wide sleeves and side slits are based on a Chinese robe. The rose motif appeals to European tastes yet uses traditional Japanese techniques.

This smart **Victorian hat** is made from elegant pearl grey straw plait, trimmed with ribbon and ostrich feathers. In the 19th century, millions of exotic birds were killed for their feathers for the fashion industry.

Collector Lieutenant Colonel Montague believed these **pottery owls** to be an ancient Greek vessel, made about 2,500 years ago. It is actually a Moche vessel from Peru in South America, made almost 1,000 years later than he thought.

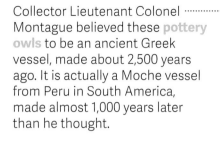

This is a carved wooden figure of **Eshu**. In the Yoruba religion, Eshu enforces the will of the Creator and helps those in need. Eshu was known as a trickster, and Christians associated him with the Devil. This may be why the word 'idol' is painted on him.

DID YOU KNOW?

The flints on display are just a few of over 200,000 found by retired teacher Nan Pearce in fields near Honiton. Nan walked the fields for over 50 years and her collection tells the story of the lives of Devon's early hunter-gatherer and farming communities through the flint tools they left behind.

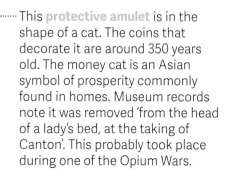

This **protective amulet** is in the shape of a cat. The coins that decorate it are around 350 years old. The money cat is an Asian symbol of prosperity commonly found in homes. Museum records note it was removed 'from the head of a lady's bed, at the taking of Canton'. This probably took place during one of the Opium Wars.

Discovering Worlds

Oceania is the name given to the many island cultures of the central and southern Pacific Ocean. It includes Australia and the three regions defined in the 19th century as Polynesia, Melanesia and Micronesia. There are many distinct cultures and identities in these islands. We refer to their inhabitants as Oceanic peoples.

Many of RAMM's artefacts were acquired from early European voyages, missionary work, trade and colonial activity in the Pacific. Ongoing collections research adds to our knowledge of the artefacts and the dynamic, thriving culture of Oceanic peoples.

World Cultures

RAMM's World Cultures gallery focuses on the lives of traditional communities in Africa, North and South America, Asia and the islands of the Pacific Ocean.

Many of the objects in World Cultures were brought to Exeter by men who travelled abroad in the 19th century as traders, missionaries and explorers, or who served as British soldiers, sailors and colonial administrators. We don't always know the circumstances in which these objects were acquired. Some were purchased or received as gifts, others may have been taken by force.

In the 19th century, European collectors often showed little respect for the culture and religious beliefs of people who were not white and not Christians. They did not acknowledge that certain objects, materials or patterns had a special or sacred meaning. In recent years, the museum has returned human remains and some artefacts to their original communities.

During the 20th and 21st centuries, traditional communities have been affected by technology, globalisation and other changes. The objects in RAMM's rich and diverse World Cultures collection provide a powerful sense of connection with past and present communities across the world.

Blackfoot ceremonial elder Herman Yellow Old Woman gave this **regalia** to RAMM in 2022. It took him three years to make. He tanned the hide and applied the intricate beadwork himself.

DID YOU KNOW?

The World Cultures displays contain over 800 artefacts from many parts of the world. However, this represents only 7% of RAMM's ethnography collection.

This early ceremonial **Congolese drum** depicts a priestess communicating with the ancestors. It states on the drum that it was acquired from a temple, but it probably came from a shrine. It was donated to RAMM by a Dartmouth shipbuilder named Richard Redway.

This kind of **battle-hammer** is extremely rare. The carved head is in the form of a stylised flying fox fruit bat - an animal eaten by some and revered as a god by others in pre-Christian Fiji. Similar high-status weapons are made in the form of owls and snakes. They were probably used by the gods to enter and leave a priest's body in pre-Christian possession rites.

This is a cast of an **Oba** (king of Benin) on horseback. A Yoruba artist made it around 1968 using the lost wax technique. It is in the Benin court style made for sale to a British expatriate.

Polynesian artist Rosanna Raymond made these **barkcloth-decorated jeans** in February 2007. Barkcloth represents identity and status, and is often used in ceremony. It is culturally significant for Pacific islanders and its manufacture is part of a preserved tradition.

Tahitian chiefs were considered powerful individuals imbued with great spiritual power. To mourn their death, a senior relative wore an elaborate costume to lead a spectacular procession. This **Tahitian mourner's costume** was acquired in 1792 by Francis Godolphin Bond during the second breadfruit voyage.

This **samurai armour** (tosei gosuku) was made in Japan after 1500. It was unlikely to have been worn in battle. The suit is composed of pieces from two different suits. The armour is made of lacquered metal plates laced with gold-coloured silk braid.

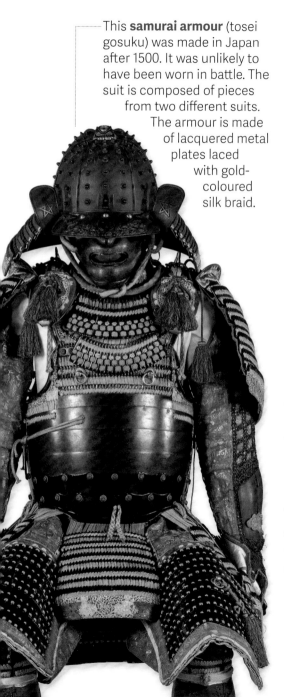

Golden Fields of Rice is a vessel made by lacquer master Matsumi Suzuki in 2009. Suzuki employed a technique called maki-e, which is the process of incorporating gold-leaf into layers of transparent lacquer that are painted upon the thin wood.

This rare 18th-century **deerskin riding coat** (casacón) comes from Veracruz, Mexico. It was owned by a very wealthy landowner (hacendado), but was acquired by Exeter resident Edward Burton Penny, a trader in the jalap medicinal root. Penny's grandfather was James Penny, a mariner who made his fortune trafficking enslaved people.

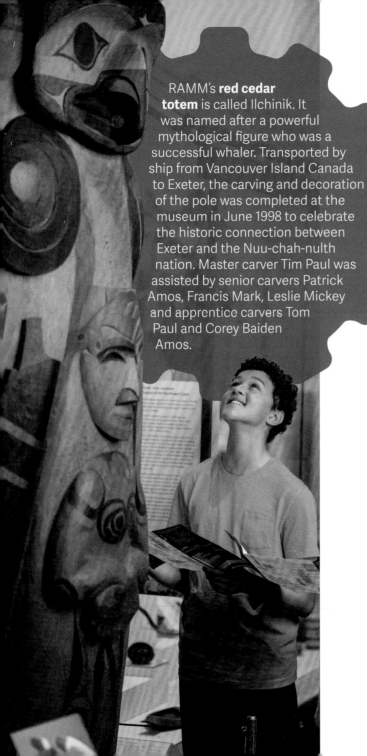

RAMM's **red cedar totem** is called Ilchinik. It was named after a powerful mythological figure who was a successful whaler. Transported by ship from Vancouver Island Canada to Exeter, the carving and decoration of the pole was completed at the museum in June 1998 to celebrate the historic connection between Exeter and the Nuu-chah-nulth nation. Master carver Tim Paul was assisted by senior carvers Patrick Amos, Francis Mark, Leslie Mickey and apprentice carvers Tom Paul and Corey Baiden Amos.

Nuu-chah-nulth master carver Joe David made this **cedar rattle**. It comes from the Northwest Coast, Canada, and portrays shamanic transformation. A human face is carved on one side and a seal's face on the reverse.

Tim Paul received it as a gift. Tim and his family carved Ilchinik (RAMM's totem pole) and, in accordance with the Nuu-chah-nulth tradition of gift-giving, he gave the rattle to museum volunteer Graeme Searle. Graeme and Tim became good friends and he invited Graeme to help decorate the totem pole. In 2017 RAMM bought the rattle from Graeme's family.

Ancient Worlds

The Ancient Worlds gallery presents a fascinating selection of objects that were made and used by people who lived thousands of years ago in the Mediterranean region and Middle East.

Much later, explorers and treasure-hunters rediscovered ancient sites in Mesopotamia (present-day Iraq), Egypt, Cyprus, Greece and the territories of the Roman Empire. When they uncovered unusual and intriguing artefacts, they often took them home, without recording essential information about where and when they were found.

Some 19th-century archaeologists were more careful to document their discoveries. They set the scene for modern archaeology, which gives us a more accurate picture of the ancient Mediterranean world and its people. These days, most archaeological finds stay in the country where they were excavated.

Ancient civilisations helped to shape our lives today. 'Democracy' is an ancient Greek idea. Our coins still look similar to the coins the Romans used. In Exeter and elsewhere, you'll find town halls, banks and other buildings that resemble Greek and Roman temples.

The Egyptian Tomb display contains the coffin and mummified body of **Shep en-Mut**. We treat this area of the museum with special respect.

Some of the hieroglyphics on the coffin tell us that Shep en-Mut was the daughter of Nesamenopet, carrier of the milk jar of Amun at the Temple of Thebes. She lived over 2,800 years ago.

The Pegasus (winged horse) was a popular mythical creature in ancient Greece. Lieutenant Colonel Montague purchased this 2,300-year-old **Pegasus plate** from a collector named Harold Clemens who set up a museum in his public house.

DID YOU KNOW?

The ancient Egyptians thought that mice were born from mud because when the River Nile flooded all of the mice rushed from the fields. Cats were seen as sacred but even mice were sometimes mummified.

This **bronze Roman mouse** is one of the smallest exhibits in the gallery. Mice were as common in Roman houses as they are in ours. This little figure was used as a toy or to remind the owner to live life as simply as a mouse.

This **Hoplite helmet** may have been worn by a Greek warrior to fight the Persian armies at the Battle of Marathon 2,500 years ago. It made the warrior look fearsome but must have been very difficult to see out of. They were only safe to wear when fighting in a phalanx, a tightly-packed group of spearmen.

Sladen's Study

Step back in time to when exploration of the deep seas had just begun. The 70,000 nautical mile voyage of HMS *Challenger* (1872-76) laid the foundations for almost every branch of ocean science we know today. It proved that life not only existed at great depth, but it thrived. The voyage collected thousands of species new to European science. Many would not have been seen by a human before.

Percy Sladen (1849-1900) dedicated his life to the study of Echinoderms – a group of sea creatures including starfish, sea urchins and their relatives. He was a world expert. Percy contributed nearly 1,000 pages and 118 drawings to the final 50-volume report on the specimens collected by HMS *Challenger* – how many specimens can you find in this gallery?

Percy amassed a huge collection of books and over 5,000 specimens from all over the world including microscope slides and fossils. It is thought to be the largest and most comprehensive Echinoderm collection in the UK outside the Natural History Museum, London.

Walter Percy Sladen, known as Percy.

In life, starfish and sea urchins are beautiful colours – purples, reds, yellows and oranges. Preservation in alcohol bleaches **specimens** over time leaving them creamy-white.

Starfish collected by the HMS *Challenger* Expedition in the Torres Strait, Australia, 9 September 1874.

Look closely and you will see that some specimens aren't what they seem. Inspired by Sladen's collection, contemporary glass artist Steffen Dam created **Specimens from an Imaginary Voyage** especially for RAMM. Made entirely of glass these delicately coloured sea forms look almost like real animals.

Percy's wife **Constance** was among the first women to join the Linnean Society of London in 1904. Initially women were not allowed in Britain's scientific societies, preventing them from fully participating in scientific study. She donated Percy's collection to RAMM and paid for this gallery to be created.

In Fine Feather

Measure your wingspan against an albatross. Find the smallest bird in the world. Marvel at a lyre bird. Experience the sharp end of a raptor's talons. This dazzling array of over 140 birds showcases the diversity of species in RAMM's bird collection.

In the past, collectors brought specimens back from their travels and mounted them for display as symbols of wealth and status. Collected for their impressive feathers, vibrant colours or rarity they came to RAMM from 30 different countries. Today, many of these species are protected by law. Newer additions to RAMM's collections are the result of accidental death, poor weather or they were captive birds.

Take a quiet moment, how many bird calls do you recognise?

After seeing a cast of **Archaeopteryx** at RAMM in June 1915, the English writer Thomas Hardy was inspired to write the poem *In a Museum*. He imagined how the bird's song may have sounded, '... a contralto voice I heard last night, That lodges with me still in its sweet singing.'

Great bustard are one of the heaviest birds capable of flight. They used to live in Britain but humans hunted them to extinction in the 19th century. In 2004, great bustard from Europe and Asia were released in Wiltshire. There are now over 100 birds breeding there.

The **kākāpō** or owl parrot is one of the most endangered birds in the world. In July 2022 just 252 birds were left. These nocturnal parrots are only found in New Zealand. They cannot fly and so they make burrows in the ground.

Joey the **Stanley crane** lived at the Royal Botanic Gardens in Kew for over 20 years. Kew's records note his love affair with a female paradise crane, him losing a toe in a lawn mower accident and his courage protecting a flock of storks from bullying geese.

Fly on the Wall

Six legs, three main body parts, two antennae and sometimes one or two pairs of wings. Only a few components, yet insects look so different from one another. This gallery showcases the astounding diversity in the insect world from the tiniest moth to the largest beetle. Some are perfectly camouflaged to blend in with their natural environment. Others have vibrant colours and can be seen from a great distance.

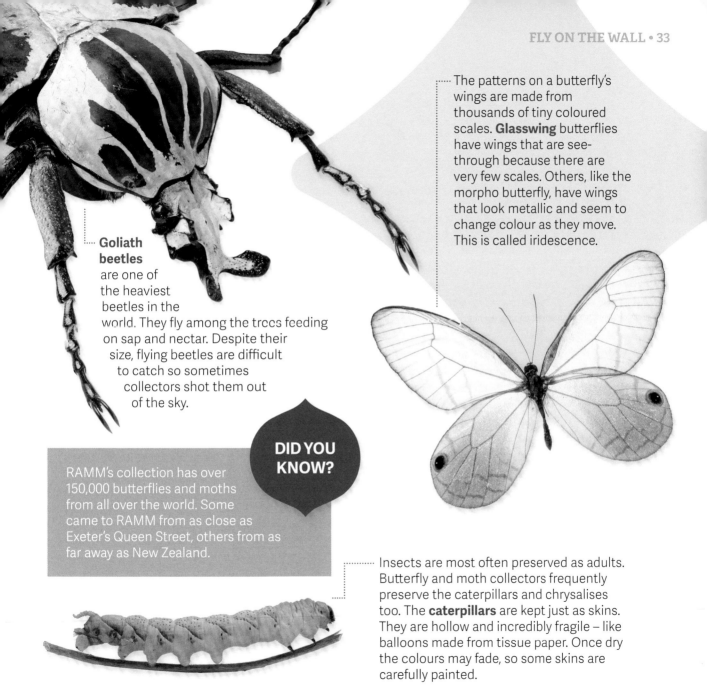

The patterns on a butterfly's wings are made from thousands of tiny coloured scales. **Glasswing** butterflies have wings that are see-through because there are very few scales. Others, like the morpho butterfly, have wings that look metallic and seem to change colour as they move. This is called iridescence.

Goliath beetles are one of the heaviest beetles in the world. They fly among the trees feeding on sap and nectar. Despite their size, flying beetles are difficult to catch so sometimes collectors shot them out of the sky.

DID YOU KNOW?

RAMM's collection has over 150,000 butterflies and moths from all over the world. Some came to RAMM from as close as Exeter's Queen Street, others from as far away as New Zealand.

Insects are most often preserved as adults. Butterfly and moth collectors frequently preserve the caterpillars and chrysalises too. The **caterpillars** are kept just as skins. They are hollow and incredibly fragile – like balloons made from tissue paper. Once dry the colours may fade, so some skins are carefully painted.

Down to Earth

This gallery takes you on a journey through millions of years. It begins when the Earth was a very different place, and Exeter and Devon did not look like they do today. Devon's landscape was formed by huge natural forces and later by people's actions. Rest by a fossil seabed and watch the passage of time unfold before your eyes.

Rocks and fossils tell the story of Devon's natural history from the early coral seas around 409 million years ago to the last ice age. Some animals are perfectly preserved, each bone, scale and tooth. Others leave only traces, such as footprints in the sand.

Many of the objects in this gallery show the way people have interacted with Devon's rich geology. For centuries, Devon's mineral wealth supported thriving industries. Tin was mined in large quantities as well as arsenic, china clay and iron. Two or three hundred years ago Devon produced two-thirds of the world's copper. Stone quarried in Devon can still be seen in Exeter's buildings, including RAMM. These extraction industries changed Devon's landscape forever.

120 million years ago, **hippos** and straight-tusked elephants roamed the swampy land near Honiton. Road workers found their fossilised remains while constructing the Honiton Bypass in 1968.

A nearly complete fossilised skeleton of a juvenile **ichthyosaur** – a name derived from the ancient Greek for fish lizard. This predator swam in the seas during the Triassic and Jurassic periods, over 250 million years ago. The fossil was found at Lyme Regis, Dorset.

Cheilichnus bucklandi was a reptile about the size of a small dog. A set of fossilised footprints made in damp desert sand are the only trace of *Cheilichnus*. Its skeleton has never been found.

Making History

Making History tells the story of people's lives in Devon and Exeter, from the earliest settlers 12,000 years ago to our own times. The story unfolds through all kinds of objects that connect us to the people who made, used and owned them. You'll find treasures and tools, clothes and pictures, weapons, toys and mystery objects.

Many of these objects once belonged to chieftains, landowners or wealthy merchants. Poorer people left few possessions, but they are just as much part of our story. When archaeologists excavate a rubbish pit, they'll often uncover evidence of both poor and rich people's lives.

Exeter's history has many ups and downs. It was a flourishing Roman city, then a ghost town. Later, it was home to traders and merchants who became rich by selling woollen cloth. During the Industrial Revolution, Exeter's fortunes dipped again. By the late 19th century, it had become a popular tourist destination.

In the Second World War, Exeter was devastated by bombing. When the city was rebuilt, centuries of history were revealed under the High Street. As archaeologists make fresh discoveries, our understanding of the past grows and changes.

There are an incredible 22,888 Roman coins in the **Seaton Down Hoard**. They weigh over 68kg. What a wallet they would have needed!

Kingsteignton figure, dating to the Iron Age. This wooden figure is a very rare find; only a few others are known from Britain. It was found quarrying clay in 1867. Its purpose is unclear. Was it a toy or a religious artefact buried to appease the gods?

This brocaded **silk gown** features a design of trees and pretty, meandering ribbons. The skilful, three-dimensional flowers created by the weaver and braidmaker enliven an otherwise formal garment. It was made between the 1750s and 1770s and was passed down through the Pennell family, landowners from Dawlish.

DID YOU KNOW?

Some objects are particularly sensitive to light. The costume and textiles on display are changed regularly to prevent them from fading.

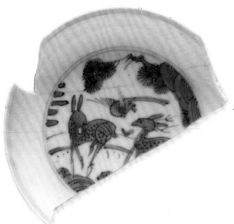

You can't miss the **model of Exeter**. It took Caleb Hedgeland over seven years to make in the 1820s. It is the only one of its kind in the country.

Exeter's Tudor merchants grew rich on international trade. They used their wealth to bring luxury goods from all around the world, including pottery from Germany, France, Holland, Spain, Portugal and Italy as well as Islamic glass. This **Ming Chinese porcelain dish** was made around 1590.

This type of Second World War air-raid shelter is known as an **Anderson shelter**. It would either have been installed inside a house or buried under the soil in the garden. This one comes from Woodville Road, St Thomas, Exeter. It was later used as a garden shed until it was donated to the museum in the 1990s.

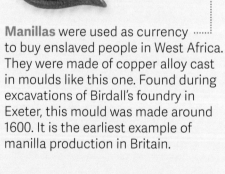

This Late Medieval **stained glass angel** wears a feathered suit and holds an incense burner known as a censer. The style is very similar to glass in the Chapter House at Exeter Cathedral.

Manillas were used as currency to buy enslaved people in West Africa. They were made of copper alloy cast in moulds like this one. Found during excavations of Birdall's foundry in Exeter, this mould was made around 1600. It is the earliest example of manilla production in Britain.

Henry Ellis was an Exeter silversmith. His work often used silver from the Combe Martin mines on Exmoor. In 1851 he exhibited a new **brooch** at the Great Exhibition. Its innovative design, which he patented, features a safety chain to make sure the brooch could not fall off.

········ The **Exeter puzzle jug** was
made in France around 1300.
It is an incredible example of
the potter's skill and the medieval
imagination. What is that strange
beast that forms the spout and are
there really naked bishops in the tower?

RAMM's Fine Art

RAMM's Fine Art collection is rich and varied. Over 7,000 paintings, prints, drawings, watercolours, miniatures, photographs and sculptures date from the 1400s to the present day. The gallery themes are curated around time, people and place. The displays change regularly to showcase the breadth of RAMM's collections.

RAMM has collected Fine Art since the 1860s. It has always relied on the generosity of supporters including trusts, foundations and individuals to help purchase new works. Many of the most famous and popular works in the collection have come to the museum as a result of its supporters' efforts.

Looking back over a century shows how fashion and taste have played their part in collecting art. Acquisitions in the earlier 20th century were dominated by figurative works with historical or classical subjects. In the latter decades of the century the work of living artists breathed new life into the collection. A constant has been acquiring works capturing the changing face of Exeter and Devon.

From time to time this gallery may be used for other exhibitions.

Portrait of a Man in a Red Suit, artist and sitter unknown, oil on canvas, mid 18th century. There have been many discussions about this painting's subject since it came into RAMM's collections in the 1940s. In the past it was thought to show Olaudah Equiano or Ignatius Sancho, once enslaved people who had significant roles in London society.

Apple Blossom, Riversbridge Farm, Blackpool by Lucien Pissarro, oil on canvas, 1921. This view depicts one of Pissarro's favourite locations in south Devon.

The Fair Toxophilites (or English Archers, Nineteenth Century) by William Powell Frith, oil on canvas, 1872. This work depicting young archers (toxophilites) was created as a fanciful representation of the artist's three daughters. It has become one of the most famous images of affluent Victorian leisure.

The interior of Exeter Cathedral by Thomas Girtin, pencil and watercolour on paper, 1797. Girtin captured this accomplished view of the cathedral on one of his tours of the South West. It includes valuable details on the cathedral interior before the 19th-century renovations.

Artists inspired by RAMM

From *Specimens from an Imaginary Voyage* by Steffen Dam, inspired by the sea creatures in Sladen's Study, to Michelle Williams Gamaker's film *The Silver Wave*, made in response to RAMM's Arctic collections, visitors are sure to find new and exciting art interspersed among the museum's displays.

The historic collections cared for by RAMM provide the inspiration for artists working in a wide range of media to create thought-provoking new work. Paintings by Maria Lalic, inspired by the museum's geological collections, were an integral element of the 2011 redevelopment project and work by renowned artists from the UK and beyond is regularly incorporated into galleries.

Inspiration for recent artists' commissions has included birds, seaweeds and seeds. *Aerial* a video work created by Heinrich and Palmer, was first shown in a RAMM exhibition on bird migration. Bryony Gillard's moving-image work *Unctuous Between Fingers* was shown alongside seaweeds collected by Victorian women on local beaches. Photographer Léonie Hampton's series of family and friends in her vegetable garden was displayed with seeds from RAMM's collection in the exhibition *A Language of Seeds*.

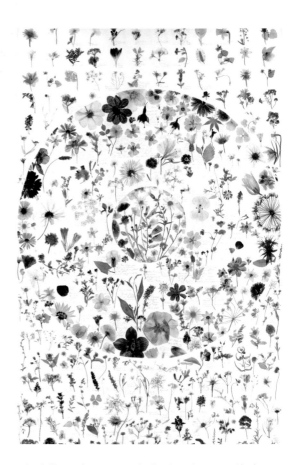

Biophilia – The Exeter Florilegium by Amy Shelton was commissioned by RAMM during the first Covid-19 lockdown. Shelton's work is a herbarium of pressed plant specimens collected on her daily lockdown walks around the Royal Devon & Exeter Hospital.

Phizogs by award-winning artist Bedwyr Williams was commissioned by RAMM to celebrate the museum's 150th anniversary. Williams installed giant faces from the collection in RAMM's iconic Victorian foyer.

Joy Gregory was commissioned to work with the museum collections and local people to explore RAMM's relationship to the trans-atlantic slave trade for a major exhibition. Her work, *The Sweetest Thing* was acquired for the museum collection. Gregory, who was born to Jamaican parents, made the tapestry after seeing a depiction of a Black child in an 18th-century tapestry.

Detail from *The Sweetest Thing* by photographer and artist Joy Gregory.

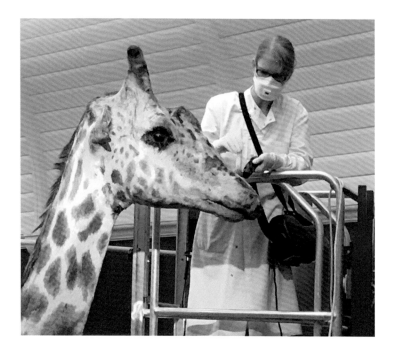

Behind the scenes

RAMM has long been recognised for the quality of its diverse collections. The museum's role is to preserve these important historical assets for future generations, so they can enjoy and learn from them just as much as you can. The museum's in-house conservation and technical team are responsible for taking care of objects whether on display or in store.

A conservator or technician has prepared each object you see in the museum. Much of their work is almost invisible. It can include cleaning and repairing an object or making a bespoke display mount.

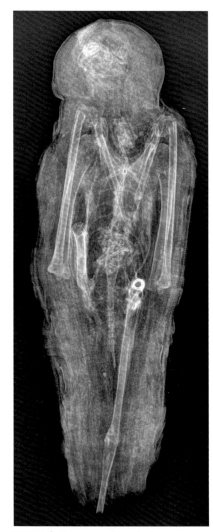

RAMM's X-ray machine helps curators and conservators identify archaeological objects, and see hidden structures inside. This X-ray shows an ancient Egyptian bird mummy.

A lot of thought goes into the treatment of each object. What is it made from? What has caused damage to it? How is it possible to stop further deterioration? What is the object's history and does this affect its treatment?

Another significant aspect of collections care is monitoring and controlling the environment around an object. This includes temperature, humidity and light levels which can all cause damage if they are too high or too low. It also includes the type of packaging material that surrounds an object and stopping pests from munching objects, particularly ones made from wool and plant fibre.

Any conservation treatment is carefully documented, and together with all the other information held about an object, they are filed on RAMM's collections database. With over one million objects at RAMM, the database is crucial in finding information and the location of an object quickly and easily.

Temporary exhibitions

RAMM has special galleries for temporary exhibitions, so that visitors can enjoy all sorts of nationally important art and artefacts loaned to Exeter. The themes for temporary exhibitions reflect RAMM's rich collections and a range of issues relevant to the contemporary world.

In recent years, RAMM has curated a number of landmark exhibitions showcasing the South West and its distinctive sense of place. They have drawn on the museum's own collections supplemented by major loans and commissioned artworks.

Sea Life: Glimpses of the Wonderful introduced visitors to the world of Philip Henry Gosse, a Victorian biologist whose work in Devon pioneered and popularised studies of marine life. *Sea Garden* brought together the work of living artists exploring the theme of the sea and seaweed, starting with the story of RAMM's Victorian seaweed collectors. *By Royal Appointment: Devon's lace-makers* investigated the real lives of the local men and women who provided fashionable Victorian women with East Devon lace. And RAMM's *In Plain Sight: Transatlantic slavery and Devon* scrutinised and exposed local links to the trade in enslaved Africans in the 18th century.

It's not only in the special exhibition galleries that displays change. RAMM regularly replaces the contents of the boxes in the Courtyard gallery to show more examples from the collection.

BIRDS OF PASSAGE

RAMM's exhibitions offer something for all ages. *Birds Without Borders* featured contemporary art, handling opportunities and specimens to explore the science and folklore of bird migration.

RAMM's dementia-friendly activities were inspired by New York's Museum of Modern Art (MoMA). It's all about living in the moment.

There's a growing international movement for museums to nurture visitors' wellbeing, through mindful activities and calm spaces to pause.

Did you know that the sparkling cloth under the elephant-headed god Ganesh was hand-sewn and donated by Exeter Hindu Cultural Centre? Local communities breathe life into the collections.

This museum likes dressing up - and down! Dig through the wardrobe for a Time Travellers' Ball or contemplate a life drawing class or a pub quiz at one of our eclectic *Lates* events.

RAMM in the community

Is it real? Is it alive? Enjoy the challenge of curious questions that pop up when children of all ages explore RAMM. Families gawp, talk and play around the galleries. Discover interactive corners, with costumes to flounce in and fossils to touch.

Has someone smiled at you today? RAMM reaches out to new visitors, from local estates to the latest arrivals in town, playgroups to care homes. A day at the museum is a chance to spend time side by side, experiencing the moment together.

Let an object spark a new conversation. A busy team of volunteers brings history to life for thousands of Devon schoolchildren, while museum displays and guided workshops inspire creative ideas for artists of all ages and abilities.

There are quiet spaces to nourish the soul, and places to make music. Incredible objects connect RAMM to so many places and people. Listen to the stories woven into them. Dance to your own tune, and show us the steps.

You're never too young to enjoy a museum.

So many untold stories. RAMM's objects mean different things to different people.

RAMM has level access throughout the building. The museum tries to smooth out the stress of a day by working with and for Deaf and disabled visitors and artists. You can borrow ear defenders, print out a visual guide, or see online tours in British Sign Language (BSL).

History of Exeter

Exeter is one of Britain's oldest cities. It began in about AD 55 when the Roman army constructed a fortress overlooking the river Exe. The town that grew up was Isca Dumnoniorum, or simply Isca. Parts of Exeter's Roman city walls are still standing but the fortress now lies hidden below the modern city centre and a once luxurious bath-house is underneath Cathedral Green.

But as Rome's power declined, people deserted Exeter. Its buildings were ruined and the land was used for farming. Later, they gradually returned. A church was built within the walls, and in 1050 bishop Leofric moved his seat from Crediton to Exeter, bringing cathedral status. After the Norman Conquest a castle was constructed at Rougemont and a new bridge spanned the Exe. You can see parts of both still standing.

By the Middle Ages, Exeter was a busy manufacturing and trading hub. The Guildhall stood on the same spot it still occupies today. In the 1500s Devon's woollen cloth became popular and local merchants grew prosperous on exports from the quay. Their townhouses can still be admired in South Street and High Street. It was called a 'Golden Age' although many residents were poor.

By the mid-1600s Exeter was England's fifth largest city.

The South Gate, Exeter drawn by Thomas Rowlandson, ink, pencil and watercolour on paper, 1805. Before it was dismantled in 1819, Exeter's South Gate was one of the grandest medieval town gates standing in southern England.

Roman amphora. This so-called 'carrot amphora' actually contained preserved fruit from Palestine in the eastern Mediterranean. The soldiers from Isca could have the finest foods from around the Roman world sent to them.

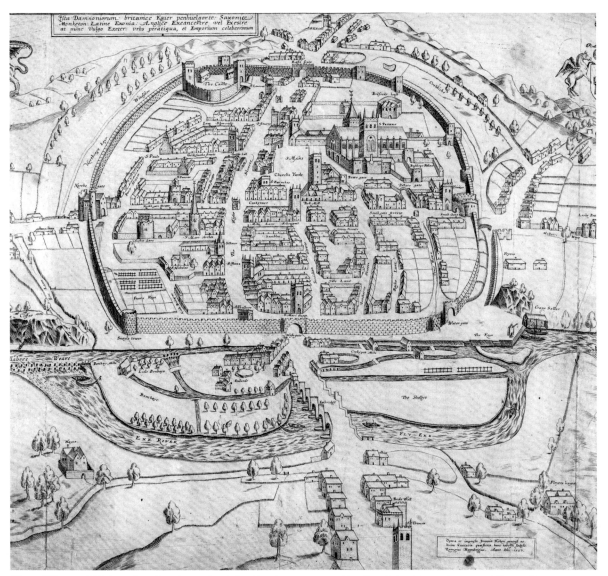

Plan of Exeter / Civitas Exoniae drawn by John Hooker, engraved by Remigius Hogenberg and Georg Braun. Produced in 1587, this was the first widely produced 'map' of Exeter. In fact, it's actually a bird's-eye view of the Tudor city.

EXETER: THE QUAY. The Custom House is in back red (local) brick with plaster bressings. The buildings shown in front form two sides of the square (Custom House on N; Harbour Master office E.) Roofs and slate-hanging in the tall building behind the Harbour Master office are of Devonshire slate. Custom House windows sashed in two on left. Royal Arms & Arms of the City of Exeter in relief. Pink represents sand stone retaining-walling and containing.
John Piper

The Quay, Exeter by John Piper, watercolour and collage. Piper's artwork shows the Custom House, which is associated with Exeter's historic woollen cloth industry. The image was featured in an article of 1944. However, Piper may have made the work on an earlier trip.

In the Industrial Revolution, Devon's cloth traders lost out to competitors closer to coal deposits. While Exeter relied on water power, mills in the midlands and northern England were driven by steam. But the lack of polluting industry meant Exeter retained its beauty and tranquillity. The city became a base for visitors to coast and countryside.

Exeter Cathedral, The Great Crater, 1942 by Dennis Flanders, watercolour and charcoal on paper. This view in the aftermath of bombing shows the devastation around the cathedral.

EXETER   CO-OPERATIVE   SOCIETY   LIMITED
EXTENSION   TO   CENTRAL   PREMISES

Design for Co-operative Society Building, Eastgate by the architect W.J. Reed in about 1940.
As was typical for the period, the design was influenced by the Art Deco movement.

Some families enjoyed their holidays so much they stayed. Population growth in the early 1800s led to bigger suburbs at St Thomas and St Leonard's, and the village of Heavitree grew closer to Exeter. When the first railway arrived at St David's station in 1844, even more people were encouraged to visit. By the time of the First World War Exeter was known as a lively centre for shopping and leisure.

Exeter's centre was devastated by bombing in 1942. Historic buildings were gutted by fire and then demolished. Bedford Circus, a fine example of Georgian architecture and the medieval church of St Lawrence were destroyed. After the war, the city centre was rebuilt. The Princesshay area was transformed in the early 21st century by a modern shopping centre which stands in sharp contrast to the red sandstone of the historic buildings.

The modern city of Exeter has a population of about 130,000 people.

Acknowledgements and credits

Page 11 *Curtius leaping into the Gulf* - Purchased with support from the Kent Kingdon Bequest.

Page 22 *Golden Fields of Rice* - Purchased with support from the Art Fund.

Page 23 *Cedar rattle* - Purchased with support from V&A Purchase Grant Fund and the Friends of RAMM.

Page 29 *Specimens from an Imaginary Voyage* - The commission was made possible with support from the Art Fund, the National Lottery through Arts Council England and the Friends of RAMM.

Page 38 *Seaton Down Hoard* - RAMM acquired the coins with help from a generous donation by Patrick and Sally Long, Clinton Devon Estates, Thomson Reuters, Devon County Council and many members of the public. Patrick and Sally Long were particularly keen that the coins are preserved for inspiration and wonder of children. The conservation and display of the hoard and a project to engage with East Devon schools and communities was funded by a grant from the Heritage Lottery Fund with further public donations.

Page 40 *Stained glass angel* - Purchased with support from the V&A Purchase Grant Fund, the Art Fund, the Friends of RAMM and the Kent Kingdon Bequest.

Page 43 *The Fair Toxophilites* - Purchased with support from the V&A Purchase Grant Fund and the Sir Harry Veitch Bequest Trust Fund.

Page 43 *Apple Blossom* - Purchased with support from the Reynolds Chard Bequest and the MLA/V&A Purchase Grant Fund.

Page 43 *The interior of Exeter Cathedral* - Purchased with support from Art Fund, the Friends of RAMM and the Kent Kingdon Bequest

Page 44 *Biophilia* - Commissioned by RAMM and purchased with support from Arts Council England, the Arts Council England/V&A Purchase Grant Fund, the Friends of RAMM and the Kent Kingdon Bequest.

Page 45 *The Sweetest Thing* - Presented by the Contemporary Art Society with support from Arts Council England and the Friends of RAMM.

Page 52 *The South Gate, Exeter* - Purchased with support from the MLA/V&A Purchase Grant Fund, the Art Fund, the Friends of RAMM and the Kent Kingdon Bequest.

Page 54 *The Quay, Exeter* - Purchased with support from the Art Fund, Arts Council England/V&A Purchase Grant Fund and the Friends of RAMM.

Designed by Jamieson Eley.
Text by the RAMM team and Michael Bird

JARROLD
publishing

Published by Jarrold Publishing
www.jarrold-publishing.co.uk